# New Poems

# NEW POEMS | Günter Grass

In German with translations by

Michael Hamburger

A Helen and Kurt Wolff Book

Harcourt, Brace & World, Inc., New York

# Contents

# New Poems

## Ausgefragt

Nach grossem und nach kleingemünztem Zorn,—
beliebtes Beispiel, dem man Zucker gab,—
nach soviel Damals und dem Salto
auf einem Hochseil, das periodenlang
gespannt war,—Arbeit ohne Netz,—
will, will ich, will ich ganz und gar . . .
   Wie sieht es aus?—Es sah schon schlimmer aus.
   Du hattest Glück?—Es lag am Köder.
   Und was hast du gemacht seitdem?
   In Büchern steht, wie es sich besser machte.
   Ich meine, was hast du getan?
   Ich war dagegen. Immer schon dagegen.
   Und wurdest schuldig?—Nein. Ich tat ja nichts.
   Und hast erkannt, was sich erkennen liess?
   Ja. Ich erkannte Gummi mit der Faust.

   Und deine Hoffnung?—Log die Wüsten grün.
   Und deine Wut?—Sie klirrt als Eis im Glas.
   Die Scham?—Wir grüssen uns von fern.
   Dein grosser Plan?—Zahlt sich zur Hälfte aus.
   Hast du vergessen?—Neuerdings, mein Kopf.
   Und die Natur?—Oft fahr ich dran vorbei.
   Die Menschen?—Seh ich gern im Film.
   Sie sterben wieder.—Ja. Ich las davon . . .
Wer seift mich ab? Mir ist mein Rücken
so fern wie—Nein!—
ich will nicht mehr vergleichen
und widerkäuen, Silben stechen
und warten, bis die Galle schreibt.
   Ist es jetzt besser?—Es sieht besser aus.
   Soll ich noch fragen?—Frag mich aus.

# Questioned

About the large and the small coin of anger,—
popular instance that was fed with sugar,—
after so much At That Time and the leap
up on a tightrope that whole periods long
was tautened,—work without a net,—
I will, with all my heart, I will . . .
    How do things look?—They have looked worse.
    You were in luck?—It was the bait.
    And what have you been doing since?
    In books you'll find out how it should be done.
    I mean, what have you done?
    I was against it. Always, from the start.
    And so are guilty?—No, since I did nothing.
    And you have learnt all that there was to learn?
    Yes. With my fist I learned what rubber is.

    And hope? Your hope?—It lied the deserts green.
    Your rage?—As ice it clatters in the glass.
    And shame?—We greet each other, from a distance.
    Your major project?—Isn't worth all that much.
    Have you forgotten?—Lately, yes, my head.
    And nature?—Often I drive past it.
    Your fellow men?—I like to see them filmed.
    Once more they're dying.—Yes, I've read about it.
Who soaps and washes me? My back feels far
From me as—No!—
Enough of that. Enough of similes,
chewing the cud and splitting hairs,
of waiting for my gall to write.
    Well, is that better?—It looks better now.
    More questions?—Yes, continue. Pump me dry.

## Zwischen Greise gestellt

Wie sie mit neunzig noch lügen
 und ihren Tod vertagen,
  bis er Legende wird.

In die fleckigen Hände
 frühaufstehender Greise
  wurde die Welt gelegt.

Die vielgefältete Macht
 und der Faltenwurf alter Haut
  verachten die Glätte.

Wir, zwischen Greise gestellt,
 kauen die Nägel knapp,
  wir wachsen nicht nach.

Hart, weise und gütig
 dauern sie in Askese
  und überleben uns bald.

## Placed amid Old Men

How at ninety they still lie
  and put off their dying
    till it's a legend.

Into the mottled hands
  of old men who rise early
    the world was laid.

Their many times folded power
  and the folds of old skin
    despise what is smooth.

Placed amid old men, we
  bite our nails till they're spare,
    we make no new growth.

Hard, wise and kind
  they last ascetically
    and soon will outlive us.

# Ehe

Wir haben Kinder, das zählt bis zwei.
Meistens gehen wir in verschiedene Filme.
Vom Auseinanderleben sprechen die Freunde.
Doch meine und Deine Interessen
berühren sich immer noch
an immer den gleichen Stellen.
Nicht nur die Frage nach den Manschettenknöpfen.
Auch Dienstleistungen:
Halt mal den Spiegel.
Glühbirnen auswechseln.
Etwas abholen.
Oder Gespräche, bis alles besprochen ist.
Zwei Sender, die manchmal gleichzeitig
auf Empfang gestellt sind.
Soll ich abschalten?
Erschöpfung lügt Harmonie.
Was sind wir uns schuldig? Das.
Ich mag das nicht: Deine Haare im Klo.
Aber nach elf Jahren noch Spass an der Sache.
Ein Fleisch sein bei schwankenden Preisen.
Wir denken sparsam in Kleingeld.
Im Dunkeln glaubst Du mir alles.
Aufribbeln und Neustricken.
Gedehnte Vorsicht.
Dankeschönsagen.
Nimm Dich zusammen.
Dein Rasen vor unserem Haus.
Jetzt bist Du wieder ironisch.
Lach doch darüber.
Hau doch ab, wenn Du kannst.
Unser Hass ist witterungsbeständig.

## Marriage

We have children, that counts up to two.
We usually go to different films.
It's friends who talk of our drifting apart.
   But your interests and mine
   still touch, at the same points always.
   Not only the question about cufflinks.
   Little services too:
   Just hold that mirror.
   Change the bulbs.
   Fetch something.
   Or discussions, till everything is discussed.
Two stations that at times
are both tuned in to receive.
Shall I turn myself off?
   Exhaustion simulates harmony.
   What do we owe each other? That.
   I don't like that—your hairs in the john.
But after eleven years the thing is still fun.
To be one flesh when prices fluctuate.
We think thriftily, in small coin.
In the dark you believe all I say.
Unpicking and knitting anew.
A stretched cautiousness.
Saying thank you.
   Pull yourself together.
   That lawn of yours in our garden.
   Now you're being ironic again.
   Why don't you laugh about it?
   Clear out, then, if you can.
   Our hatred is weatherproof.

Doch manchmal, zerstreut, sind wir zärtlich.
Die Zeugnisse der Kinder
müssen unterschrieben werden.
  Wir setzen uns von der Steuer ab.
  Erst übermorgen ist Schluss.
  Du. Ja Du. Rauch nicht so viel.

But sometimes, distrait, we are tender.
The children's reports
have to be signed.
    We deduct each other from income tax.
    Not till the day after tomorrow will it be over.
    You. Yes, you. Don't smoke so much.

# Advent

Wenn Onkel Dagobert wieder die Trompeten vertauscht,
und wir katalytisches Jericho mit Bauklötzen spielen,
weil das Patt der Eltern
oder das Auseinanderrücken im Krisenfall
den begrenzten Krieg,
also die Schwelle vom Schlafzimmer zur Eskalation,
weil Weihnachten vor der Tür steht,
nicht überschreiten will,
    wenn Onkel Dagobert wieder was Neues,
    die Knusper—Kneisschen—Maschine
    und ähnliche Mehrzweckwaffen Peng! auf den Markt wirft,
    bis eine Stunde später Rickeracke . . . Puff . . . Plops!
    der konventionelle, im Kinderzimmer lokalisierte Krieg
    sich unorthodox hochschaukelt,
und die Eltern,
weil die Weihnachtseinkäufe
nur begrenzte Entspannung erlauben,
und Tick, Track und Trick,—
das sind Donald Ducks Neffen,—
    wegen nichts Schild und Schwert vertauscht haben,
    ihre gegenseitige, zweite und abgestufte,
    ihre erweiterte Abschreckung aufgeben,
    nur noch minimal flüstern, Bitteschön sagen,
wenn Onkel Dagobert wieder mal mit den Panzerknackern
und uns, wenn wir brav sind, doomsday spielt,
weil wir alles vom Teller wegessen müssen,
weil die Kinder in Indien Hunger haben
und weniger Spielzeug und ABC-Waffen,
die unsere tägliche Vorwärtsverteidigung
vom Wohnzimmer bis in die Hausbar tragen,
in die unsere Eltern das schöne Kindergeld stecken,
bis sie über dreckige Sachen lachen,

# Advent

When Uncle Dagobert again swaps trumpets
and we play catalytic Jericho with wooden bricks
because the stalemate between our parents
or their disengagement in crisis periods
does not want to exceed
limited war,
that is, the threshold between bedroom and escalation,
because Christmas is at the door,
    when Uncle Dagobert again throws something new,
    the crackle and crunch machine
    and such-like all-purpose weapons Bang! on to the market
    till an hour later Whizzbuzz . . . Puff . . . Plop!
    conventional war, localized in the nursery,
    unorthodoxly flares up
    and our parents
    because the Christmas shopping
    permits only limited relaxation of tension
    and Huey, Dewey and Louie,—
    those are Donald Duck's nephews,—
    for no reason have swapped shields and swords,
    give up their reciprocal, second
    and gradual deterrent, only
    minimally whisper now, and say please,
when Uncle Dagobert again with the safe-crackers
and with us, if we're good, plays doomsday,
because we have to eat up everything on our plates
because the children in India go hungry
and have fewer toys and ABC weapons
which carry our daily forward defence
from the drawing-room up to the house bar
on which our parents spend all that lovely children's allowance
until they laugh about their dirty jokes,

kontrolliert explodieren
und sich eigenhändig,
wie wir unseren zerlegbaren Heuler,
zusammensetzen können,
    wenn ich mal gross und nur halb so reich
    wie Onkel Dagobert bin,
    werde ich alle Eltern, die überall rumstehen
    und vom Kinder anschaffen und Kinder abschaffen reden,
    mit einem richtigen spasmischen Krieg überziehen
    und mit Trick, Track und Tick,—
    das sind die Neffen von Donald Duck,—
    eine Familie planen,
    wo bös lieb und lieb bös ist
    und wir mit Vierradantrieb in einem Land-Rover
    voller doll absoluter Lenkwaffen
    zur Schule dürfen,
    damit wir den ersten Schlag führen können;
denn Onkel Dagobert sagt immer wieder:
Die minimale Abschreckung hat uns bis heute,—
und Heiligabend rückt immer näher,—
keinen Entenschritt weiter gebracht.

restrainedly explode
and with their own hands, as we can
our make-it-yourself siren,
can put themselves together again,
    when I'm grown up and half as rich
    as Uncle Dagobert,
    I shall plunge all those parents who everywhere
    stand around and talk of getting children
    and getting rid of children, into a real spasmic war
    and with Huey, Dewey and Louie,—
    those are Donald Duck's nephews,—
    I shall plan a family
    in which naughty is good and good naughty
    and we can go to school
    with a four-wheel drive in a Land Rover
    full of smashing all-in guided missiles
    so that we can strike the first blow;
for Uncle Dagobert is always saying:
Up to now the minimal deterrent,—
and Christmas Eve is drawing closer and closer,—
hasn't got us a duck's step further, has it now?

## Plötzliche Angst

Wenn sich im Sommer bei östlichem Wind
  Septemberstaub rührt und in verspäteter Zeitung
  die Kommentare Mystisches streifen,

wenn sich die Mächte umbetten wollen
  und zur Kontrolle neue Geräte
  öffentlich zeugen dürfen,

wenn um den Fussball Urlauber zelten
  und der Nationen verspielter Blick
  grosse Entscheidungen spiegelt,

wenn Zahlenkolonnen den Schlaf erzwingen
  und durch die Träume getarnter Feind
  atmet, auf Ellbogen robbt,

wenn in Gesprächen immer das gleiche Wort
  aufgespart in der Hinterhand bleibt
  und ein Zündhölzlein Mittel zum Schreck wird,

wenn sich beim Schwimmen in Rückenlage
  himmelwärts nur der Himmel türmt,
  suchen die Ängstlichen rasch das Ufer,

liegt plötzliche Angst in der Luft.

## Sudden Fright

When in summer in an easterly wind
   September dust whirls and in the belated paper
    editorials are almost mystical,

when the powers want to change beds
   and are allowed to beget openly
    new instruments for control,

when around footballs holiday makers camp
   and the playful glance of the nations
    mirrors weighty decisions,

when columns of figures put one to sleep
   and through dreams a camouflaged enemy
    breathes, and crawls nearer,

when in conversations always the same word
   is backhandedly held in reserve
    and a match can strike terror,

when from the backstroke position in swimming
   skyward only the sky seems to tower,
    frightened people hurry back to the shore,

a sudden fright hangs in the air.

## König Lear

In der Halle,
in jeder Hotelhalle,
in einem eingesessenen Sessel,
Klub-, Leder-, doch niemals Korbsessel,
zwischen verfrühten Kongressteilnehmern
und leeren Sesseln, die Anteil haben,
selten, dann mit Distanz gegrüsst,
sitzt er, die von Kellnern umsegelte Insel,
und vergisst nichts.

Diese Trauer findet an sich Geschmack
und lacht mit zwölf Muskeln einerseits.
Viel hört er nicht aber alles
und widerlegt den Teppich.
Die Stukkatur denkt er weg
und stemmt seine Brauen gegen.
Bis sich ihr Blattgold löst,
sprechen Barockengel vor.
Die Kirche schickt Spitzel;
ihm fehlen Komparsen.
Vergeblich ahmen zuviele Spiegel ihn nach.
Seine Töchter sind Anekdoten.

Im Hotel Sacher wird nach Herrn Kortner verlangt.
Herr Kortner lässt sagen, er sei auf der Probe.
In der Halle, in seinem Sessel, stellt jemand sich tot
und trifft sich mit Kent auf der Heide.

# King Lear

In the hall
in any hotel hall
in a chair that sags with long use,
club, leather but never basket chair,
amid premature participants in congresses
and empty armchairs that play their part,
rarely addressed and, if so, with reserve,
he sits,
an island skirted by cruising waiters,
and forgets nothing.

This grief takes pleasure in itself
and laughs with twelve muscles on the one side.
He does not hear much but everything
and refutes the carpet.
His mind rips off the stucco work
and his eyebrows push it away.
Till their gold leaf peels off
baroque angels present themselves.
The church sends informers;
what he lacks is walk-ons.
In vain too many mirrors copy him.
His daughters are anecdotes.

In Hotel Sacher Herr Kortner is paged.
Herr Kortner is busy rehearsing, he has them say.
In the hall, in his armchair, someone acts dead
and goes to meet Kent on the heath.

## Vom Rest unterm Nagel

Wovon erzählen, immer noch vom Knopf
und Bodensatz, der übrig blieb,
von Aschenbechern, Sound and Light,
was übrig blieb, was überblieb,
vom Zinsertrag der kleinen Konten
und von der Zeit, die uns geblieben?

Wovon erzählen, von der Liebe?
Wovon? Noch immer von der Liebe?
Wovon, als ob nur Liebe zählt
und jeder nicht mit seinem Kot allein
auf jedem Abtritt einzeln steht,
mit Fingernägeln: ganz allein.

Das kratzt sich offen, heilt sich nicht
und speichert Reste unterm Nagel:
ich trenn mich nicht, ich putz sie nicht
und weise alle harten Instrumente
zurück: denn Liebe geht mit Geiz
zu Tisch zu Bett und wäscht sich nicht.

Wovon, wenn von der Liebe nicht?
Vom Vorrat, wenn wir fleissig sind,
vom fetten schwarzen abverdienten Rest
will ich erzählen, wenn wir fertig sind
und unsre Nägel, zweimalzehn,
vom Augentauschen dreckig sind.

# Of the Residue under Our Nails

Talk about what now, still about the button
and dregs, deposits left behind,
about the ashtrays, Sound and Light,
whatever stayed, was left behind,
the interest rate on small accounts,
about the time we still have left?

Talk about what now, about love?
What? About love still? Even now?
Of that? As though love only counted
And every one of us were not alone
each morning only with his turd,
with fingernails, and quite alone.

This is scratched open, does not heal,
and under nails hoards residues:
I will not part with, will not clean them
and I refuse sharp instruments,
all kinds: for love with avarice goes
to meals to bed and does not wash.

Well, of what else then, if not love?
Of savings, if we work our stint,
of that black, greasy hard-earned residue
I'll talk when we have finished work
and when those nails of ours, twice ten,
are foul with intercourse of eyes.

## Offenes Feuer

Ein leeres Haus im Rücken,
  und die Gewissheit trocknender Strümpfe;
    draussen mühen sich ab altbekannte Gewitter.

Mit imprägnierten Gedanken
  in fremder Glut, später in Asche
    stochern; denn die erwärmte Seite hat recht.

Genüsse und schöne Gespräche
  mit dem erregten schreckhaften Holz;
    ich lasse mich leicht überreden.

Das lebt vor sich hin, bis. Mach,
  nun mach schon die Tür zu.
    Drinnen wird alles wirklich.

Die früher bewohnten Kamine
  wurden schon gestern geräumt.
    Morgen, kopfunten, hängt kalter Rauch.

## Open Fire

An empty house behind me,
   and the certainty of drying socks;
      outside, familiar thunderstorms exert themselves.

With waterproofed thoughts
   to poke about in a strange ardour, later
      in ashes; for the warm side is in the right.

Pleasures and fine conversations
   with the excited timorous wood:
      I am easily persuaded.

This quietly lives on, until. Shut,
   will you please shut the door.
      Inside, all becomes real.

The previously inhabited fireplaces
   were already cleaned out yesterday.
      Tomorrow, head down, cold smoke will hang.

## Schlaflos

Mein Atem verfehlte das Nadelöhr.
Jetzt muss ich zählen
und heimwärts blättern treppab.

Aber die Kriechgänge
münden in Wassergräben,
in denen Kaulquappen . . .
Zähl doch mal nach.

Meine Rückspule plappert ihr drittes Jahrzehnt.
Das Bett geht auf Reisen. Und überall legt
der Zoll seine Hand auf: Was führen sie mit?

Drei Strümpfe, fünf Schuhe, ein Nebelgerät.—
Mehrsprachig werden sie nachgezählt:
die Sterne, die Schafe, die Panzer, die Stimmen . . .
Ein Zwischenergebnis wird ausgezählt.

## Sleepless

My breath missed the needle's eye.
Now I must count
and homeward leaf down the stairs.

But the crawling forays
end in watery ditches,
in which tadpoles . . .
Count up again.

My playback reel gabbles its third decade.
The bed leaves for a journey. And everywhere
The Customs interpose: What's in your luggage?

Three socks, five shoes, a fog machine.—
In several languages they are counted up:
the stars, the sheep, the tanks, the voices . . .
A provisional sum is counted out.

## Liebe

Das ist es:
Der bargeldlose Verkehr.
Die immer zu kurze Decke.
Der Wackelkontakt.

Hinter dem Horizont suchen.
Im Laub mit vier Schuhen rascheln
und in Gedanken Barfüsse reiben.
Herzen vermieten und mieten;
oder im Zimmer mit Dusche und Spiegel,
im Leihwagen, Kühler zum Mond,
wo immer die Unschuld absteigt
und ihr Programm verbrennt,
fistelt das Wort
jedesmal anders und neu.

Heute, vor noch geschlossener Kasse,
knisterten Hand in Hand
der gedrückte Greis und die zierliche Greisin.
Der Film versprach Liebe.

# Love

That's it:
The cashless commerce.
The blanket always too short.
The loose connection.

To search behind the horizon.
To brush fallen leaves with four shoes
and in one's mind to rub bare feet.
To let and to rent hearts;
or in a room with shower and mirror,
in a hired car, bonnet facing the moon,
wherever innocence stops
and burns its programme,
the word in falsetto sounds
different and new each time.

Today, in front of a box office not yet open,
hand in hand crackled
the hangdog old man and the dainty old woman.
The film promised love.

## Dreht euch nicht um

Geh nicht in den Wald,
im Wald ist der Wald.
Wer im Wald geht,
Bäume sucht,
wird im Wald nicht mehr gesucht.

Hab keine Angst,
die Angst riecht nach Angst.
Wer nach Angst riecht,
den riechen
Helden, die wie Helden riechen.

Trink nicht vom Meer,
das Meer schmeckt nach mehr.
Wer vom Meer trinkt,
hat fortan
nur noch Durst auf Ocean.

Bau dir kein Haus,
sonst bist du zuhaus.
Wer zuhaus ist,
wartet auf
spät Besuch und macht auf.

Schreib keinen Brief,
Brief kommt ins Archiv.
Wer den Brief schreibt,
unterschreibt,
was von ihm einst überbleibt.

## Don't Turn Round

Don't go into the wood,
in the wood is the wood.
Whoever walks in the wood,
looks for trees,
will not be looked for later in the wood.

Have no fear,
fear smells of fear.
Whoever smells of fear
will be smelled out
by heroes who smell like heroes.

Don't drink from the sea,
the sea tastes of more sea.
Whoever drinks from the sea
henceforth feels
a thirst only for oceans.

Don't build a home,
or you'll be at home.
Whoever is at home
waits for
late callers and opens the door.

Don't write a letter,
letters that vex us end up in Texas.
Whoever writes the letter
lends his name
to the posthumous paper game.

## Platzangst

Mama. Sie kommen auf mich zu
und knacken mit den Handgelenken,
die Söhne aus zu gutem Haus.

So wohlerzogen nimmt Gewalt
den Anlauf, nett, studentenhaft,
mit Kussmundfragen: Glauben Sie?
ein nackter Finger: Hoffen Sie?
die Drohung zielt, zum Schlips gebunden,
als Zusatzfrage: Lieben Sie?

Jetzt lockern sie den Knoten, jetzt:
Mitesser überlebensgross.
Die Söhne aus zu gutem Haus.

Es ist so schön hier, auch bei Regen.
An Zigaretten glaub ich immer noch.
Mein Schnittlauch grünt, die Hoffnung auch.
Und manchmal, wenn ich mich zerstreue,
kehrt mich die Liebe mit Geduld aufs Blech.

Mama. Es hat sich Heiterkeit
verflogen und ist überfällig.
Eng wird es zwischen Ideologen
und Söhnen aus zu gutem Haus.
Sie kommen näher. Ich will raus.

## Claustrophobia

Mother. They're coming up to me
and ominously crack their wrists,
those boys from families too good.

So well brought up does violence
run to the start, so public school,
so nice, caressing: Do you believe?
a naked finger: Do you hope?
the threat, a necktie neatly knotted,
aims as a supplement: Do you love?

And now the knot is loosened, now:
blackheads much more than life-size, bloated.
Those boys from families too good.

A lovely place, even in rainy weather.
I still believe in cigarettes, don't you?
My chives are green and thriving, so is hope.
And sometimes, when I seek distraction,
love sweeps me on the dustpan patiently.

Mother. This cheerfulness has flown
too far and now is overdue.
They're closing up—the ideologists
and boys from families too good.
They're coming nearer. Let me out.

# Hymne

So kompliziert wie eine Nachtigall,
so blechern wie,
gutmütig wie,
so knitterfrei, althergebracht,
so grün ernst sauer, so durchwachsen,
so ebenmässig,
so behaart,
so nah dem Wasser, windgerecht,
so feuerfest, oft umgegraben,
so kinderleicht, zerlesen wie,
so neu und knarrend, teuer wie,
so unterkellert, häuslich wie,
so leicht verloren, blankgegriffen,
so dünn geblasen, schneegekühlt,
so eigenhändig, mündig wie,
so herzlos wie,
so sterblich wie,
so einfach wie meine Seele.

# Hymn

As complicated as a nightingale,
as tinny as,
kind-hearted as,
as crease-proof, as traditional,
as green grave sour, as streaky,
as symmetrical,
as hairy,
as near the water, true to the wind,
as fireproof, frequently turned over,
as childishly easy, well-thumbed as,
as new and creaking, expensive as,
as deeply cellared, domestic as,
as easily lost, shiny with use,
as thinly blown, as snow-chilled as,
as independent, as mature,
as heartless as,
as mortal as,
as simple as my soul.

# Orpheus

Weil ich mich damals zum Publikum zählte,
nahm ich Platz in der siebzehnten Reihe.
So, die Hände überm Programm,
hielt ich es aus bis kurz nach der Pause:

den Kapellmeister strich ich durch,
dem Klavier ins Gebiss, der Flöte ein Auge
weg und das Blech gefüllt,—womit denn?—mit Blei.
Es galt, die Hälfte aller Instrumente zu enthaaren.

Wer schnitt mir damals den Film ab?
Platzanweiser bekamen Gewalt,
warfen mich Geigen vor, Hemdbrüsten,
was von Noten schwarz-weiss lebt, liniert.

Die Harfenistin, trotzdem ein Weib,
beugte sich über mich, trug ein mildtätig Kleid.
So ging ich in ihre Saiten ein,
verstehe mich nur noch auf Finger:

Wohlklang, ich überhöre mich, hüte mich,
nach ihrem Programm zu verlangen.

## Orpheus

Because at that time I thought myself part of the public
I took a seat in the seventeenth row.
Like that, my hands on the programme,
I stuck it out till shortly after the intermission.

I cancelled the conductor with one bold stroke,
aimed at the piano's denture, put out one eye
of the flute and filled the brass—with what, then?—with lead.
To depilate half the instruments, that's what was needed.

Who cut my film at that time?
Ushers were given power,
hurled me down before violins, shirtfronts,
all that of notes lives black and white, ruled.

The harpist, a woman all the same,
bent over me, wore a charitable dress.
So I passed over into her strings,
an adept now only in fingers:

Euphony, I listen to myself, beware
of asking for her programme.

## Der Dampfkessel-Effekt

Immer zum Zischen bereit.
Schneller gezischt als gedacht.
Nicht mehr mit Fäusten,
zischend wird argumentiert.
Bald wird es heissen:
Er wurde zu Tode gezischt.
Aber noch lebt er und spricht.
Auf seine Frage gab Zischen Antwort.
Seht dieses Volk, im Zischen geeint.
Zischoman. Zischoplex. Zischophil.
Denn das Zischen macht gleich,
kostet wenig und wärmt.
Aber es kostete wessen Geld,
diese Elite, geistreich und zischend,
heranzubilden.
Als wollte Dampfablassen
den nächstliegenden Nero bewegen,
jeweils den Daumen zu senken.
Pfeifen ist schön. Nicht jeder kann pfeifen.
Dieses jedoch, anonym,
macht ängstlich und lässt befürchten . . .

## The Steam Boiler Effect

Always ready to hiss.
Sooner hissed than thought.
No longer with fists
people argue, but hissing.
Soon they will say:
He was hissed to death.
But still he's alive and speaks.
His questions were answered by hisses.
Look at this people, united in hissing.
Hissomaniac. Hissoplex. Hissophile.
For hissing is a leveller,
costs little and keeps warm.
But it costs whose money,
to train
this élite, witty and hissing.
As though letting off steam
could move the local Nero
to the thumb-down sign every time.
Whistling is fine. Not anyone can whistle.
But this thing, anonymous,
is worrying and makes one fear . . .

# In Ohnmacht gefallen

Wir lesen Napalm und stellen Napalm uns vor.
Da wir uns Napalm nicht vorstellen können,
lesen wir über Napalm, bis wir uns mehr
unter Napalm vorstellen können.
Jetzt protestieren wir gegen Napalm.
    Nach dem Frühstück, stumm,
    auf Fotos sehen wir, was Napalm vermag.
    Wir zeigen uns grobe Raster
    und sagen: Siehst du, Napalm.
    Das machen sie mit Napalm.
Bald wird es preiswerte Bildbände
mit besseren Fotos geben,
auf denen deutlicher wird,
was Napalm vermag.
Wir kauen Nägel und schreiben Proteste.
    Aber es gibt, so lesen wir,
    Schlimmeres als Napalm.
    Schnell protestieren wir gegen Schlimmeres.
    Unsere berechtigten Proteste, die wir jederzeit
    verfassen falten frankieren dürfen, schlagen zu Buch.
Ohnmacht, an Gummifassaden erprobt.
Ohnmacht legt Platten auf: ohnmächtige Songs.
Ohne Macht mit Guitarre.—
Aber feinmaschig und gelassen
wirkt sich draussen die Macht aus.

## Powerless, with a Guitar

We read napalm and imagine napalm.
Since we cannot imagine napalm
we read about napalm until
by napalm we can imagine more.
Now we protest against napalm.
   After breakfast, silent,
    we see in photographs what napalm can do.
   We show each other coarse screen prints
   and say: there you are, napalm.
   They do that with napalm.
Soon there'll be cheap picture books
with better photographs
which will show more clearly
what napalm can do.
We bite our nails and write protests.
   But, we read, there are
   worse things than napalm.
   Quickly we protest against worse things.
   Our well-founded protests, which at any time
   we may compose fold stamp, mount up.
Impotence, tried out on rubber façades.
Impotence puts records on: impotent songs.
Powerless, with a guitar.—
But outside, finely meshed
and composed, power has its way.

# Irgendwas machen

Da können wir doch nicht zusehen.
Wenn wir auch nichts verhindern,
wir müssen uns deutlich machen.
(Mach doch was. Mach doch was.
Irgendwas. Mach doch was.)
Zorn, Ärger und Wut suchten sich ihre Adjektive.
Der Zorn nannte sich gerecht.
Bald sprach man vom alltäglichen Ärger.
Die Wut fiel in Ohnmacht: ohnmächtige Wut.
Ich spreche vom Protestgedicht
und gegen das Protestgedicht.
(Einmal sah ich Rekruten beim Eid
mit Kreuzfingern hinterrücks abschwören.)
Ohnmächtig protestiere ich gegen ohnmächtige Proteste.
Es handelt sich um Oster-, Schweige- und Friedensmärsche.
Es handelt sich um die hundert guten Namen
unter sieben richtigen Sätzen.
Es handelt sich um Guitarren und ähnliche
die Schallplatte fördernde Protestinstrumente.
Ich rede vom hölzernen Schwert und vom fehlenden Zahn,
vom Protestgedicht.

Wie Stahl seine Konjunktur hat, hat Lyrik ihre Konjunktur.
Aufrüstung öffnet Märkte für Antikriegsgedichte.
Die Herstellungskosten sind gering.
Man nehme: ein Achtel gerechten Zorn,
zwei Achtel alltäglichen Ärger
und fünf Achtel, damit sie vorschmeckt, ohnmächtige Wut.
Denn mittelgrosse Gefühle gegen den Krieg
sind billig zu haben
und seit Troja schon Ladenhüter.
(Mach doch was. Mach doch was.
Irgendwas. Mach doch was.)

# Do Something

We can't just look on.
Even if we can't stop anything
we must say what we think.
(Do something. Do something.
Anything. Do something, then.)
Indignation, annoyance, rage looked for their adjectives.
Indignation called itself righteous.
Soon people spoke of everyday annoyance.
Rage fell into impotence: impotent rage.
I speak of the protest poem
and against the protest poem.
(Once I saw recruits taking the oath
unswear it behind their backs with crossed fingers.)
Impotently I protest against impotent protests.
What I mean is Easter, silence and peace marches.
What I mean is the hundred good names
underneath seven true sentences.
What I mean is guitars and similar
protest instruments conducive to records.
I speak of the wooden sword and the missing tooth,
of the protest poem.

Just as steel has its booms, so poetry has its booms.
Rearmament opens markets for anti-war poems.
The cost of production is low.
Take an eighth of righteous indignation,
two eighths of everyday annoyance
and five eighths—to heighten that flavour—of impotent rage.
For medium-sized feelings against the war
are cheaply obtained
and have been shopsoiled ever since Troy.
(Do something. Do something.
Anything. Do something, then.)

Man macht sich Luft: schon verraucht der gerechte Zorn.
Der kleine alltägliche Ärger lässt die Ventile zischen.
Ohnmächtige Wut entlädt sich, füllt einen Luftballon,
der steigt und steigt, wird kleiner und kleiner, ist weg.
Sind Gedichte Atemübungen?
Wenn sie diesen Zweck erfüllen,—und ich frage,
prosaisch wie mein Grossvater, nach dem Zweck,—
dann ist Lyrik Therapie.
Ist das Gedicht eine Waffe?
Manche, überarmiert, können kaum laufen.
Sie müssen das Unbehagen an Zuständen
als Vehikel benutzen:
sie kommen ans Ziel, sie kommen ans Ziel:
zuerst ins Feuilleton und dann in die Anthologie:
Die Napalm-Metapher und ihre Abwandlungen
im Protestgedicht der sechziger Jahre.
Es handelt sich um Traktatgedichte.
Gerechter Zorn zählt Elend und Terror auf.
Alltäglicher Ärger findet den Reim auf fehlendes Brot.
Ohnmächtige Wut macht atemlos von sich reden.
(Mach doch was. Mach doch was . . .)
Dabei gibt es Hebelgesetze.
Sie aber kreiden ihm an, dem Stein,
er wolle sich nicht bewegen.
Tags drauf ködert der hilflose Stil berechtigter Proteste
den treffsicheren Stil glatter Dementis.
Weil sie in der Sache zwar jeweils recht haben,
sich im Detail aber allzu leicht irren,
distanzieren sich die Unterzeichner
halblaut von den Verfassern und ihren Protesten.
(Nicht nur Diebe kaufen sich Handschuhe.)
Was übrig bleibt: zählebige Missverständnisse

One lets off steam: already righteous indignation goes up in smoke.
The small everyday annoyance makes the safety valves hiss.
Impotent rage discharges itself, fills a balloon with gas,
this rises, rises, grows smaller and smaller, is gone.
Are poems breathing exercises?
If that is their function,—and prosaic
as my grandfather, I ask what their function is—
then poetry is therapy.
Is a poem a weapon?
Some, too heavily armed, can hardly walk.
They have to use their dissatisfaction with circumstances
as a vehicle:
they reach their destination, they can hit the mark:
first the weekly paper, then the anthology:
The napalm metaphor and its permutations
in the protest poem of the 'sixties.
I mean poems that are tracts.
Righteous indignation enumerates terrors and miseries.
Everyday annoyance discovers the rhyme for no bread.
Impotent rage sets people talking breathlessly about itself.
(Do something. Do something . . .)
There are laws of leverage.
But they hold it against the stone
that it will not budge.
Next day the helpless style of well-founded protest
acts as a bait for the well-aimed style of smooth refutation.
Since in the cause they are always right
but all too easily slip up over details
the signatories tacitly half-dissociate themselves
from the authors and from their protests.
(Not only burglars buy gloves.)
What remains is: resilient misunderstandings

zitieren einander. Fehlerhafte Berichtigungen
lernen vom Meerschweinchen
und vermehren sich unübersichtlich.

Da erbarmt sich der Stein und tut so,
als habe man ihn verrückt:
während Zorn, Ärger und Wut einander ins Wort fallen,
treten die Spezialisten der Macht
lächelnd vor Publikum auf. Sie halten fundierte
                              Vorträge
über den Preis, den die Freiheit fordert;
über Napalm und seine abschreckende Wirkung;
über berechtigte Proteste und die erklärliche Wut.
Das alles ist erlaubt.
Da die Macht nur die Macht achtet,
darf solange ohnmächtig protestiert werden,
bis nicht mehr, weil der Lärm stört,
protestiert werden darf.—
Wir aber verachten die Macht.
Wir sind nicht mächtig, beteuern wir uns.
Ohne Macht gefallen wir uns in Ohnmacht.
Wir wollen die Macht nicht; sie aber hat uns.—
Nun fühlt sich der gerechte Zorn missverstanden.
Der alltägliche Ärger mündet in Schweigemärsche,
die zuvor angemeldet und genehmigt wurden.
Im Kreis läuft die ohnmächtige Wut.
Das fördert den gleichfalls gerechten Zorn
verärgerter Polizisten:
ohnmächtige Wut wird handgreiflich.
Die Faust wächst sich zum Kopf aus
und denkt in Tiefschlägen Leberhaken knöchelhart.
(Mach doch was. Mach doch was . . .)
Das alles macht Schule und wird von der Macht

quote one another. Erroneous corrections
learn from guinea pigs
how to breed so that no one keeps track.

The stone takes pity and acts
as though it had been moved:
while indignation, annoyance and rage interrupt one another,
the specialists in power
appear smiling in front of the public. They make well-informed
                                                  speeches
about the price demanded for freedom:
about napalm and its deterrent effects;
about well-founded protests and understandable rage.
All this is permitted.
Since power respects only power
impotent protest is allowed to carry on
until, because the noise is disturbing,
protest is no longer allowed.—
But we despise power.
We are not powerful, we keep assuring each other.
Without power we enjoy our impotence.
We do not want power; but power has us.—
Now righteous indignation feels misunderstood.
Our everyday annoyance ends in silence marches
that have first been announced and permitted.
Our impotent rage runs around in circles.
This provokes the equally righteous indignation
of angered policemen:
impotent rage becomes aggressive.
The fist grows into a head
and thinks in terms of low blows hooks to the liver knuckle-hard.
(Do something. Do something . . .)
All this becomes institutionalized, and by power

gestreichelt geschlagen subventioniert.
Schon setzt der Stein, der bewegt werden wollte,
unbewegt Moos an.
Geht das so weiter?—Im Kreis schon.
Was sollen wir machen?—Nicht irgendwas.
Wohin mit der Wut?—Ich weiss ein Rezept:

Schlagt in die Schallmauer Nägel.
Köpft Pusteblumen und Kerzen.
Setzt auf dem Sofa euch durch.
    Wir haben immer noch Wut.
    Schon sind wir überall heiser.
    Wir sind gegen alles umsonst.
    Was sollen wir jetzt noch machen?
    Wo sollen wir hin mit der Wut?
Mach doch was. Mach doch was.
Wir müssen irgendwas,
mach doch was, machen.
    Los, protestieren wir schnell.
    Der will nicht mitprotestieren.
    Los, unterschreib schon und schnell.
    Du warst doch immer dagegen.
    Wer nicht unterschreibt, ist dafür.
Schön ist die Wut im Gehege,
bevor sie gefüttert wird.
Lang lief die Ohnmacht im Regen,
die Strümpfe trocknet sie jetzt.
Wut und Ventile, darüber Gesang;
Ohnmacht, dein Nadelöhr ist der Gesang:
    Weil ich nichts machen kann,
    weil ich nichts machen kann,
    hab ich die Wut, hab ich die Wut.

is caressed beaten subsidized.
Already the stone that was to be moved
gathers moss, unmoved.
Can we go on like that?—Yes, in a circle.
What shall we do?—Not anything.
How express our rage?—I know a recipe:

Strike nails into the sound barrier.
Behead dandelions and candles.
Assert yourselves on the couch.
    We still feel rage.
    Already we're hoarse all over.
    We're against everything, vainly.
    What else can we do now?
    How shall we express our rage?
Do something. Do something.
We must do something or other,
do something, do it.
    Come on, then, quickly protest.
    That fellow won't join our protest.
    Come on, then, quickly sign.
    You've always been against it.
    Those who don't sign are for it.
Lovely is rage in the paddock,
before it is fed.
For a long time impotence ran around in the rain,
but now it is drying its socks.
Rage and safety valves, about them a song;
Impotence, your needle's eye is a song.
    Because I can't do anything,
    because I can't do anything
    I'm full of rage, I'm full of rage.

Mach doch was. Mach doch was.
Irgendwas. Mach doch was.
Wir müssen irgendwas,
hilft doch nix, hilft doch nix,
wir müssen irgendwas,
mach doch was, machen.
Lauf schweigend Protest.
Lief ich schon. Lief ich schon.
Schreib ein Gedicht.
Hab ich schon. Hab ich schon.
Koch eine Sülze. Schweinekopfsülze:
die Ohnmacht geliere, die Wut zittre nach.
Ich weiss ein Rezept; wer kocht es mir nach?

Do something, then. Do something.
Anything. Do something, then.
We must do something or other,
does no good, does no good,
we must do something or other,
do something, do it.
Silently march in protest.
Have done it once, have done it.
Write a poem, then.
Have written it, have done it.
Cook some brawn. Pig's head brawn:
let impotence jell, rage quiver in sympathy.
I know a recipe; who'll follow it cooking?

# Die Schweinekopfsülze

Man nehme: einen halben Schweinekopf
samt Ohr und Fettbacke,
lasse die halbierte Schnauze, den Ohransatz,
die Hirnschale und das Jochbein anhacken,
lege alles mit zwei gespaltenen Spitzbeinen,
denen zuvor die blaue Schlachthofmarkierung
entfernt werden sollte,
mit nelkengespickter Zwiebel, grossem Lorbeerblatt,
mit einer Kinderhand Senfkörner
und einem gestrichenen Suppenlöffel mittlere Wut
in kochendes Salzwasser,
wobei darauf zu achten ist,
dass in geräumigem Topf alle Teile
knapp mit Wasser bedeckt sind,
und der Ohrlappen, weil er sonst ansetzt,
nicht flach auf den Topfboden gedrückt wird.
  Fünf viertel Stunden lasse man kochen,
  wobei es ratsam ist, nach dem ersten Aufkochen
  mit der Schaumkelle
  die sämigen, braungrauen Absonderungen
  der inneren Schnauzenteile, sowie der Ohrmuschel
  und der halbierten leeren Hirnschale
  abzuschöpfen, damit wir zu einer klaren,
  wenn auch geschmacksärmeren Sülze kommen,
  zumal sich die rasch zum Protest gerinnende Wut,
  wie jede ohnmächtige, also eiweisshaltige Leidenschaft,
  wenn sie nicht rasch gleichmässig unterrührt wird,
  gern in weissen Partikeln dem Schaum mitteilt.
Inzwischen wiege man vier Zwiebeln
und zwei geschälte
und vom Gehäuse befreite Äpfel
möglichst klein,

## The Jellied Pig's Head

Take half a pig's head
including ear and cheek,
have the halved snout, the root of the ear,
the brainpan and the cheekbone chined,
together with two split trotters
from which the blue inspection stamp
should first have been removed,
with a clove-studded onion, a large bay leaf,
with a child's handful of mustard seed
and a level tablespoon of medium rage
place them all in boiling salt water,
taking care
that in the large pot every part
is barely covered with water
and the flap of the ear, which otherwise would stick,
is not pressed down flat on to the bottom.
   Boil gently for an hour and a quarter,
   remembering that after the first boiling-up
   it is advisable to scoop off with a ladle
   the frothy brownish-grey excretions
   from the inner part of the snout, the conch of the ear
   and the halved, empty brainpan,
   so as to obtain a pure
   though not very savoury brawn,
   particularly as the rage, which so easily curdles to protest,
   tends to communicate in white particles with the froth
   unless constantly stirred from the start.
Meanwhile chop up four onions
and two peeled
and cored apples,
preferably small,

schneide zwei Salzgurken,—
niemals Dill-, Senf- oder Delikatessgurken,—
zu winzigen Würfeln,
zerstosse in Gedanken wie im Mörser
eine gefüllte Schlüsselbeinkuhle schwarzen Pfeffer
und lasse die restliche Wut
mit beigelegter Ingwerwurzel
und wenig geriebener Zitronenschale
auf kleiner Flamme ohnmächtig ziehen.
    Sobald,—nach einer Stichprobe in die Fettbacke,—
das Kopffleisch weich ist,
die Backenzähne im Zahnbett gelockert sind,
aber noch haften,
und sich die besonders geleespendenden Hautteile
vom Ohr und an den Spalträndern
der beigelegten Spitzbeine zu lösen beginnen,
nehme man alle Teile,
sowie die nelkengespickte Zwiebel
und das Lorbeerblatt aus dem Topf,
suche mit der Schaumkelle den Topfboden
nach Knochensplittern
und den sich leicht lösenden Vorderzähnen,
sowie nach dem kiesig knirschenden Sand
der Ohrmuschel ab und lasse, während der Sud
auf kleingestelltem Feuer weiterziehen sollte,
alles auf einer Platte,
möglichst bei offenem Küchenfenster
und verengten Pupillen, abkühlen.
Jetzt gilt es, die Weichteile der Schnauze,
die Fettbacke samt eingebettetem Auge
und das darunter gelagerte Fleisch
von den Knochen zu lösen.

cut up two salted gherkins,—
never dill, mustard or vinegar pickled gherkins,—
into tiny cubes,
pound in your mind as though in a mortar
a heaped collarbone pit of black pepper
and, adding a ginger root,
as well as a little grated lemon peel,
leave the remaining rage
to simmer impotently over a low flame.
    As soon as,—after a trial jab at the cheek,—
    the meat of the head is tender,
    the back teeth are loose in the gums
    but still rooted,
    and the most jelly-conducive parts of the skin
    around the ear and the split edges
    of the added trotters begin to peel off,
    take all the components
    as well as the clove-studded onion
    and the bay leaf out of the pot,
    search the bottom with your ladle
    for bone splinters
    and the easily loosening front teeth,
    also for the grit-like grinding sand
    of the ear conch, and leave it all to cool
    on a platter,
    preferably with the kitchen windows open
    and the pupils of your eyes contracted,
    while the broth should be left to simmer
    over a low flame.
Now proceed to detach
the soft parts of the snout,
the cheek, including the eye embedded in it,
and the layers of flesh beneath them,
from the bones.

Es sei angeraten, auf weiche
bis schnittfeste Knorpelteile,
sowie auf den gallertartigen Ohrbelag,
der sich mit dem Messerrücken leichthin
vom eigentlichen Ohrlappen schaben lässt,
nicht zu verzichten,
weil gerade diese Teile,
desgleichen das lamellenförmige Zahnfleisch
und der hornige,
zur Speise- und Luftröhre leitende Zungenansatz,
unserer Sülze den speziellen
und leidenschaftlichen Sülzgeschmack geben.
Auch scheue man sich nicht,
die während der Arbeit immer wieder rasch
von einem Geleefilm überzogenen Hände
über dem dampfenden Sud abtropfen zu lassen,
weil so der Prozess des natürlichen Gelierens
abermals unterstützt wird;
denn unsere Schweinekopfsülze
soll ganz aus sich und mitgeteilter Wut,
also ohne Macht und Gelantinepapier steif werden.
Alsdann würfle man das
von den Knochen gelöste Fett und Fleisch,
desgleichen die Knorpel und Weichteile,
lege sie mit den gewiegten Zwiebeln und Äpfeln,
den winziggewürfelten Gurken,
dem gestossenen Schwarzpfeffer
und einem satten Griff Kapern in den Sud.
Mit,—nach Geschmack,—
löffelweis unterrührtem Estragonessig,—
es wird empfohlen, kräftig zu säuern,
weil Essig kalt gerne nachgibt,—

We recommend that you do not
leave out the soft
and firmer gristle
or the jelly-like covering of the ear
that can easily be scraped off with the back of a knife
from the ear flap proper,
since those very parts,
like the lamellated gums
and the horny
root of the tongue that leads to windpipe and oesophagus
impart to our brawn
that special and passionate brawn flavour.
Also, you should not fail
to let your hands, which during your work
have been covered again and again
with a film of jelly, drip dry
over the steaming broth,
because in that way the process of natural jelling
is aided once more;
for our jellied pig's head is to set
all by itself and communicated rage,
that is, without power and gelatine paper.
    Then cut up the fat and meat
    detached from the bones, not omitting the gristle,
    and together with the chopped onions and apples,
    the minutely cubed gherkins,
    the pounded black pepper,
    and an ample pinch of caper, place them in the broth.
Together with tarragon vinegar,
stirred in by the spoonful, according to taste—
we recommend a not too sparing use
because vinegar tends to weaken when cold—

lasse man alles noch einmal aufkochen,
gebe jetzt erst,
nach wenig Bedenken,
die mittlerweile
auf kleiner Flamme
schön eingedickte Wut
ohne die ausgelaugte Ingwerwurzel bei
und fülle alsdann eine zuvor
mit kaltem Wasser geschwenkte Steingutschüssel.
   Diese stelle man an einen kühlen,
   wenn möglich zugigen Ort
   und lade sich für den nächsten Abend
   freundliche Gäste ins Haus,
   die eine hausgemachte Schweinekopfsülze
   zu schätzen wissen.
Sparsamer Nachsatz: Wer ungern etwas verkommen lässt,
der lasse Grossknorpel und Knochen,
sowie die gespaltenen Spitzbeine
noch einmal auskochen,
verfeinere mit Majoran, Mohrrüben, Sellerie,
gebe, falls immer noch restliche Wut im Hause,
eine Messerspitze dazu
und gewinne so eine schmackhafte Suppe,
die, wenn man Wruken, Graupen, sonstige Kümmernisse
oder geschälte Erbsen beilegt,
kinderreichen Familien ein zwar einfaches,
aber nahrhaftes Essen zu ersetzen vermag.

bring it all to the boil once more,
only now, after brief hesitation,
adding the rage
which meanwhile
has well thickened
over a low flame,
without the drained ginger root,
and then proceed to fill
a stoneware dish previously rinsed with cold water.
  Place this in a cool,
  if possible draughty place
  and for the next night
  invite well-disposed guests
  who will appreciate
  a home-made pig's head brawn.
Thrifty postscriptum: people who don't like waste
should cook the coarse gristle and bones
as well as the split trotters
once again, for spice
adding marjoram, celery, carrots
and, provided more rage remains in the house,
a knife-tip of that,
so gaining a tasty soup
which, with turnips, barley, similar miseries
or dried peas
can replace for families with many children
a simple but nutritious meal.

# Der Epilog

Schon hat gerechter Zorn seinen Schneider gefunden.
Sonntag glättet alltäglichen Ärger.
Ach, mit der Suppe, ohnmächtig, verkochte die Wut.
Erschöpft und gezähmt sitzen wir sanft um den Tisch.
Kleine Gewinne erfreuen den Vater; Sorge will kürzen,
denn abgestimmt, Punkt für Punkt, wird unser Haushalt.
So lässt uns Fallsucht in Ohnmacht fallen.
Immer noch werden Proteste zur Kenntnis genommen
und,—auf Verlangen,—im Protokoll erwähnt.
Es liegt ein Antrag auf Unterlassung vor:
Nie mehr soll ohne Macht protestiert werden.
Stimmlos, weil nicht beschlussfähig,
vertagen wir uns auf morgen.

## The Epilogue

Already righteous indignation has found its tailor.
Sunday irons out the everyday annoyance.
Oh, with the soup, impotent rage went up in steam.
    Exhausted and tamed we gently sit round the table.
    Little gains delight Father; worries keep us short,
    for in our household point after point is put to the vote.
So falling sickness makes us fall into impotence.
Still protests are taken into consideration
and—on demand—are mentioned in the minutes.
    There is a motion for a restraining clause:
    Never again shall we protest without power.
Voiceless, because unable to constitute a quorum,
we adjourn until tomorrow.

# Neue Mystik

oder: Ein kleiner Ausblick auf die utopischen Verhältnisse
nach der vorläufig allerletzten Kulturrevolution.


Als unsere Fragebögen lückenhaft blieben
und die formierten Mächte sich ratlos näher kamen,
begann die Verschmelzung aller Systeme mit der Telepathie.

Während noch Skeptiker abseits standen,
wurden schon volkseigne Tische gerückt,
Geister gerufen, mit Hegel
und anderen Mystikern gefüttert,
bis es klopfte und leserlich Antwort gab.

Auf jener Tagung spiritistischer Leninisten in Lourdes,
deren Arbeitsgruppen das fortschrittliche Tibet
und die Errungenschaften der Therese von Konnersreuth
mit Hilfe der Schrenck-Notzing-Methode behandelten,
wurden die Vertreter aufklärender Dekadenz gemassregelt:
Fortan fiel Pfingsten auf jeweils den 1. Mai.

Im folgenden Jahr,
während der telepathischen Karwoche,
überführten Zen-Pioniere,
geleitet von den vierdimensionalen Sozial-Jesuiten,
gefolgt von indischen Kühen
und den grossen Sensitiven astraler Hindu-Kombinate,
des Stalin wächserne Leiche in Etappen nach Rom.

## New Mysticism

or: A little survey of the utopian conditions
after the temporarily ultimate cultural revolution


When our questionnaires tended to show gaps
and the established powers, puzzled, sensed a rapprochement,
all the systems began to be merged with telepathy.

While sceptics still stood aloof,
nationalized tables were turned,
spirits invoked, then fed
on Hegel and other mystics,
until there were knocks and legible answers.

At that assembly of spiritualist Leninists at Lourdes
whose working parties dealt with progressive Tibet
and the achievements of Teresa of Konnersreuth
with the aid of the Schrenck-Notzing method,
the spokesmen for enlightened decadence were called to order:
Henceforth Whitsun always fell on the first of May.

In the following year,
during the telepathic Passion Week,
Zen pioneers,
guided by the four-dimensional Socialist Jesuits
and followed by Indian cows
as well as the great sensitives of astral Hindu Corporations
transported Stalin's wax corpse by stages to Rome.

Als man, nach paladinischer Weisung,
(Eusapia Paladino, geb. 1854 in Neapel,
mediale Vorkämpferin der Neuen Mystik)
auf der windigen Insel Gotland
ein gelbhaariges Medium gefunden hatte,
wurde es zur Heldin des sozialistischen Mystizismus erklärt
und kurz nach jenem tragischen Autounfall,—
versprengte Sozialdemokraten
und marxistische Revisionisten
gestanden später den Anschlag,—
heiliggesprochen.

Die in Texas und in der Äusseren Mongolei
zwecks Umschulung an Schutzlagertischen
konzentrierten Konterrevolutionäre
nehmen fortan
von Sitzung zu Sitzung ab.

Ständig tagt unser Vollzirkel dialektischer Psychokinese.
Denn immer noch gibt die Heilige Antwort.
Um einen Tisch sitzt die Welt und holt Rat bei ihr.
Sie, die irrationale, rüstet uns ab,
sie, die telekinetische, hilft uns, das Soll zu erfüllen,
sie, die okkulte, ernährt und verwaltet uns,
nur sie, die parteiliche und unfehlbare,
sie, die gebenedeite und schmerzensreiche,
sie, die liebliche Sensitive,
füllt unsere Fragebögen,
benennt unsere Strassen,
säubert uns gründlich,
erlöst uns vom Zweifel,
nimmt uns das Kopfweh.

When, in accordance with paladinian instructions
(Eusapia Paladino, born 1854 in Naples,
medium and forerunner of the New Mysticism)
on the windy Isle of Jutland
a yellow-haired medium had been found,
she was proclaimed heroine of socialist mysticism
and shortly after that tragic motor accident,—
scattered Social Democrats
and Marxist revisionists
later confessed to the coup,—
she was canonized.

The counter-revolutionaries
concentrated in Texas and Outer Mongolia
for the purpose of re-education at the desks of protective camps
now diminish
from meeting to meeting.

Our plenary circle of dialectical psychokinesis is in permanent
                                                    session.
For still the saint answers questions.
Around one table the world sits and asks for advice.
She, the irrational, disarms us,
she, the telekinetic, helps us to fulfil the norm,
she, the occult, feeds and administers us,
only she, the partisan and infallible,
she, the blessed and sorrowful,
she, the charmingly sensitive,
fills in our questionnaires,
gives names to our streets,
cleanses us thoroughly,
delivers us from doubts,
takes away our headache.

Fortan müssen wir nicht mehr denken,
nur noch gehorchen
und ihre Klopfzeichen auswerten.

From now on we need no longer think,
only obey
and decode her knocking signals.

# Kleckerburg

Gestrichnes Korn, gezielte Fragen
verlangt die Kimme lebenslang:
Als ich verliess den Zeugenstand,
an Wände, vor Gericht gestellt,
wo Grenzen Flüsse widerlegen,
sechstausend Meter überm Mief,
zuhause, der Friseur behauchte
den Spiegel und sein Finger schrieb:
Geboren wann? Nun sag schon, wo?
  Das liegt nordöstlich, westlich von
  und nährt noch immer Fotografen.
  Das hiess mal so, heut heisst es so.
  Dort wohnten bis, von dann an wohnten.
  Ich buchstabiere: Wrzeszcz hiess früher.
  Das Haus blieb stehen, nur der Putz.
  Den Friedhof, den ich, gibts nicht mehr.
  Wo damals Zäune, kann heut jeder.
  So gotisch denkt sich Gott was aus.
  Denn man hat wieder für viel Geld.
  Ich zählte Giebel, keiner fehlte:
  das Mittelalter holt sich ein.
  Nur jenes Denkmal mit dem Schwanz
  ist westwärts und davon geritten.
Und jedes Pausenzeichen fragt;
denn als ich, zwischen Muscheln, kleckerte mit Sand,
als ich bei Brenntau einen Grabstein fand,
als ich Papier bewegte im Archiv
und im Hotel die Frage in fünf Sprachen:
Geboren wann und wo, warum?
nach Antwort schnappte, beichtete mein Stift:
  Das war zur Zeit der Rentenmark.
  Hier, nah der Mottlau, die ein Nebenfluss,

# Kleckerburg

Aimed questions, foresight well aligned
lifelong the backsight will demand:
When I had left the witness box,
stood up in court, before a wall,
where frontiers contravert the rivers,
twelve thousand feet above the smog,
at home, the barber breathed upon
his mirror, and his finger wrote:
Born when? And—out with it—born where?
    It lies to the north-east, west of,
    and still can feed photographers.
    Its name was this and now is that.
    There lived until, from then on lived.
    I spell: its name was Wrzeszcz before.
    The house still stands, but the façade.
    The graveyard, which, has ceased to be.
    Where fences were now anyone.
    Such gothic things does God think up.
    For once again at great expense.
    I counted gables, none was missing:
    The Middle Ages catch us up.
    Only that statue with the tail
    has ridden off now, has gone west.
And every station signal also asks;
for when, between small shells, I built sand castles,
when I unearthed a tombstone outside Brenntau,
when I turned over papers in the archives
and in five languages the form in the hotel:
Born when and where, block letters please, born why?
yapped for the answers, my ball pen confessed:
    It was when *Rentenmarks* were current.
    Here, by the Mottlau, a small tributary,

wo Forster brüllte und Hirsch Fajngold schwieg,
hier, wo ich meine ersten Schuhe
zerlief, und als ich sprechen konnte,
das Stottern lernte: Sand, klatschnass,
zum Kleckern, bis mein Kinder-Gral
sich gotisch türmte und zerfiel.
Das war knapp zwanzig Jahre nach Verdun;
und dreissig Jahre Frist, bis mich die Söhne
zum Vater machten; Stallgeruch
hat diese Sprache, Sammeltrieb,
als ich Geschichten, Schmetterlinge spiesste
und Worte fischte, die gleich Katzen
auf Treibholz zitterten, an Land gesetzt,
zwölf Junge warfen: grau und blind.
Geboren wann? Und wo? Warum?
Das hab ich hin und her geschleppt,
im Rhein versenkt, bei Hildesheim begraben;
doch Taucher fanden und mit Förderkörben
kam Strandgut Rollgut hoch, ans Licht.
Bucheckern, Bernstein, Brausepulver,
dies Taschenmesser und dies Abziehbild,
ein Stück vom Stück, Tonnagezahlen,
Minutenzeiger, Knöpfe, Münzen,
für jeden Platz ein Tütchen Wind.
Hochstapeln lehrt mein Fundbüro:
Gerüche, abgetretne Schwellen,
verjährte Schulden, Batterien,
die nur in Taschenlampen glücklich,
und Namen, die nur Namen sind:
Elfriede Broschke, Siemoneit,
Guschnerus, Lusch und Heinz Stanowski;
auch Chodowiecki, Schopenhauer
sind dort geboren. Wann? Warum?

where Forster roared, Hirsch Fajngold held his tongue,
where I wore out the soles of my first pair
of shoes, and being old enough to speak
learned how to stammer: sand, all clammy
for making castles, until my childhood grail
gothically towered and collapsed.
That was some twenty years after Verdun;
came thirty years of respite, till my sons
made me a father; stable smells
talk in this lilt, collector's mania
when stories, butterflies I impaled
and fished for words that cat-like trembled
on rafts of driftwood washed ashore,
gave birth to twelve, all grey and blind.
Born when? And where? Block letters please. And why?
Those questions I have dragged around,
sunk in the Rhine, buried near Hildesheim;
but divers found them and in dragging nets
flotsam and jetsam rose, were brought to light.
Beechnuts and amber, sherbet fizz,
this pen-knife and this transfer picture,
piece of a piece, ship tonnage figures,
buttons and coins and minute hands,
for every square a bag of wind.
To confidence tricks I'm driven by
my treasure trove, lost property office:
The smells, the thresholds trodden down,
debts never paid, small batteries
happy in torches, only torches,
and names that are no more than names:
Elfriede Broschke, Siemoneit,
Guschnerus, Lusch and Heinz Stanowski;
and Chodowiecki, Schopenhauer
were born there too. Born when? Born why?

Ja, in Geschichte war ich immer gut.
Fragt mich nach Pest und Teuerung.
Ich bete läufig Friedensschlüsse,
die Ordensmeister, Schwedennot,
und kennen alle Jagellonen
und alle Kirchen, von Johann
bis Trinitatis, backsteinrot.
  Wer fragt noch wo? Mein Zungenschlag
  ist baltisch tückisch stubenwarm.
  Wie macht die Ostsee?—Blubb, pifff, pschsch . . .
  Auf deutsch, auf polnisch: Blubb, pifff, pschsch . . .
  Doch als ich auf dem volksfestmüden,
  von Sonderbussen, Bundesbahn
  gespeisten Flüchtlingstreffen in Hannover
  die Funktionäre fragte, hatten sie
  vergessen, wie die Ostsee macht,
  und liessen den Atlantik röhren;
  ich blieb beharrlich: Blubb, pifff, pschsch . . .
  Da schrien alle: Schlagt ihn tot!
  Er hat auf Menschenrecht und Renten,
  auf Lastenausgleich, Vaterstadt
  verzichtet, hört den Zungenschlag:
  Das ist die Ostsee nicht, das ist Verrat.
  Befragt ihn peinlich, holt den Stockturm her,
  streckt, rädert, blendet, brecht und glüht,
  passt dem Gedächtnis Schrauben an.
  Wir wollen wissen, wo und wann.
Nicht auf Strohdeich und Bürgerwiesen,
nicht in der Pfefferstadt,—ach, wär ich doch
geboren zwischen Speichern auf dem Holm!—
in Striessbachnähe, nah dem Heeresanger
ist es passiert, heut heisst die Strasse

Yes, I was always good at history.
Ask me about the plagues and price increases.
Peace treaties fluently I can pray,
masters of orders, Swedish war,
and all the Jagellons I know,
and all the churches, from St. John's
to Holy Trinity, red brick.
  Who still asks where? My intonation
is Baltic, wily, warm as rooms.
What says the Baltic? Blubb, pfff, pshsh . . .
In German, Polish: Blubb, pfff, pshsh . . .
But when I asked the functionaries
at the assembly-weary, coach-
and-special-train-fed gathering
of eastern refugees at Hanover,
they had forgotten what the Baltic says
and made the Atlantic Ocean roar;
I kept insisting: Blubb, pfff, pshsh . . .
So: Hit him! Kill him! all yelled out,
he's turned his back on human rights,
on pensions, on his native city,
on compensations, restitutions,
just listen to his intonation:
That's not the Baltic, that's high treason.
Put screws on him and make him talk,
get wheels and tongs and pokers, blind him,
and stretch his memory on the rack.
  We want his answer: when and where.
Not on the Straw Dyke, nor in Merchants' Meadows,
nor yet in Pepper Town—would that I had
been born between great store lofts on the Holm!—
Near the small Striessbach, by the Rifle Range
it happened, and today the street

auf polnisch Lelewela,—nur die Nummer
links von der Haustür blieb und blieb.
Und Sand, klatschnass, zum Kleckern: Gral . . .
In Kleckerburg gebürtig, westlich von.
Das liegt nordwestlich, südlich von.
Dort wechselt Licht viel schneller als.
Die Möwen sind nicht Möwen, sondern.
Und auch die Milch, ein Nebenarm der Weichsel,
floss mit dem Honig brückenreich vorbei.
    Getauft geimpft gefirmt geschult.
    Gespielt hab ich mit Bombensplittern.
    Und aufgewachsen bin ich zwischen
    dem Heilgen Geist und Hitlers Bild.
    Im Ohr verblieben Schiffssirenen,
    gekappte Sätze, Schreie gegen Wind,
    paar heile Glocken, Mündungsfeuer
    und etwas Ostsee: Blubb, pifff, pschsch . . .

in Polish is called Lelewela—only
the number left of the door remains, remains.
And sand, for castles, clammy, muddy: grail  .  .  .
At Kleckerburg was born, west of.
It lies to the northwest, south of.
The light there changes much more than.
The seagulls are not seagulls, but.
And there the Milch, a Vistula tributary,
honeyed and many-bridged flowed by.
　　Baptized and vaccinated, schooled, confirmed.
　　Bomb splinters, meanwhile, were my toys.
　　And I grew up, was reared between
　　the Holy Ghost and Hitler's photograph.
　　Ships' sirens echo in my ears,
　　lopped sentences and wind-blown cries,
　　a few sound churchbells, rifle fire
　　and Baltic snatches: Blubb, pfff, pshsh  .  .  .

# Sechsundsechzig

In diesem Eidechsenjahr,—
    wirklich, auf sonnigem Putz
    atmeten viele verspielt . . .

In diesem Jahr unterwegs,—
    was mich beschleunigt, wächst,
    gibt Zeichen, hat überholt . . .

In diesem Jahr kinderleicht,—
    Jahr, das befürchten lässt: Schrott . . .

In diesem kosmischen Jahr,—
    fortschreitend witzlos verläuft . . .

In diesem Jahr auf ein Jahr,—
    Jahr ohne Gag Richtung Mond . . .

In diesem Bilderschirmjahr,—
    Eckbälle wurden verschossen,
    Schreckschüsse sassen im Tor . . .

Im sechsundsechzigsten Jahr
    tobte im Kies, zu Füssen der Mauer:
    ein unwiderrufner Befehl,
        bewegter Protest,
        ledige Wut:
        zwei Eidechsenschwänze.

## Sixty-six

In this lizard year,—
   really, on sunny plaster
      many playfully breathed . . .

In this year on my way,—
   what accelerates me, grows,
      gives me signals, has overtaken . . .

In this year childishly simple,—
   year that portends: scrap . . .

In this cosmic year,—
   progressively witlessly passes . . .

In this year for a year,—
   year without gag direction moon . . .

In this television screen year,—
   corner shots went foul,
      alarm shots struck the goal . . .

In the year sixty-six
   raged in the gravel, at the foot of the Wall:
      an order not rescinded,
         lively protest,
            sheer rage:
               two lizard tails.

## Luft holen

Seife und Äpfel kaufen.
Möwen habe ich schon beschrieben.
Diese sind kleiner.

Eisgrütze auf den Grachten igelt sich ein.
Wer hat die Mädchen
mit Graupeln beworfen: zu fettes Essen?

Man sagt, die Königin subventioniere
die Fahrräder.
Und eine der Tulpen heisst: Lustige Witwe.

Es ist schon so, dass die Zwiebel,
wenn man sie streichelt,
am Ende ja sagt.

Tagsüber lache ich vor mich hin.
Das darf man hier:
vorsichhinlachen und luftholen.

## Taking Breath

Buy soap and apples.
Seagulls—I've described them before.
These are smaller.

Ice scum on the canals curls up.
Who chucked sleet
at the girls: too rich food?

They say that the queen
subsidizes bicycles.
And one of the tulips is called Merry Widow.

It is established,
that when you stroke it the bulb
says yes in the end.

All day long I laugh to myself.
That's allowed here:
laughing to oneself and taking breath.

## Im Botanischen Garten

Die Farbenreiber leben vom Herbst.
Fünfhundert Sorten Erica,
darunter das Kräutchen Calluna der Besenheide.
　Am Sonntag Familienauftrieb:
　neben Begonien und weisser Vollendung,
　nahe dem Ricinus,
　wächst das Vivil für den übrigen Groschen,
　unseren Atem zu klären.
Nacktsamer und Farne.
Leguminosae,—unsere Liebe, Hülsenfrucht,
Scheinhasel, Zaubernuss, flüchtet sich ins Latein.—
Auf verwaschenen Schildchen
springt sie und springt
von der kanadischen Felsenbirne,
zu deren Füssen Kastanien spotten,
zum morgenländischen Lebensbaum,
der kein Laub wirft und Friedhöfen nahe steht.
　Wir lernten uns bei der blassen Miss Winett kennen.
　Im Jahre neununddreissig züchtete Otto Greul
　seine Teehybride Gretl Greul.
Wegen deiner verzweigten Verwandtschaft
stritten wir uns
unterm getüpfelten Blasenstrauch.
　Diese Rose vorm weissen Tausendschön,
　neben der kniehoch kriechenden Floribunda,
　diese Rose wurde nach einem General benannt:
　Mac Arthur. Mac Arthur. Die Rose Mac Arthur.
Nichts schreckt die Kinder,
denn zwischen Anzuchten sind alle gerollten Schlangen
sonntäglich ruhende Schläuche,
montags die Pyrenäen zu wässern,
dienstags das Amurland und so weiter . . .
　Dort, unterm Judasbaum,
　Herzblätter wirft er,
　wird eine Bank frei.

# In the Botanical Garden

The dye-makers live on autumn.
Five hundred varieties of heather,
among them the little herb calluna the ling.
    On Sundays family round-up:
    next to begonias and white perfection,
    near the ricinus,
    Mentha grows for the penny left over
    to purify our breath.
Gymnospera and ferns.
Leguminosae,—our love, edible seed,
false hazel, magic nut, takes refuge in Latin.—
On blurred little tabs
she jumps and jumps
from the Canadian rock pear
at whose foot chestnuts mock,
to the Eastern tree of life
that sheds no leaves, congenial to graveyards.
    We became acquainted at pale Miss Winett's.
    In 'thirty-nine Otto Greul grew
    his tea hybrid Gretl Greul.
Because of the distant relationship
we quarrelled
under the spotted bladder nut.
    This rose in front of the white daisies,
    next to the floribunda creeping knee-high,
    this rose was called after a general:
    MacArthur. MacArthur. The MacArthur rose.
Nothing frightens the children,
for between beds all the curled-up snakes
are hosepipes resting on Sundays,
Mondays to water the Pyrenees,
Tuesdays the land of Amur etc. . . .
    There, under the Judas tree,
    shedding heart-shaped leaves,
    a seat is being vacated.

# Vermont

Zum Beispiel Grün. In sich zerstritten Grün.
Grün kriecht bergan, erobert seinen Markt;
so billig sind geweisste Häuser hier zu haben.

Wer sich dies ausgedacht, dem fällt
zum Beispiel immer neues Grün
in Raten ein, der wiederholt sich nie.

Geräte ruhen, grünlich überwunden,
dabei war Rost ihr rötester Beschluss,
der eisern vorlag, nun als Schrott zu haben.

Wir schlugen Feuerschneisen, doch es wuchs
das neue Grün viel schneller als
und grüner als zum Beispiel Rot.

Wenn dieses Grün erbrochen wird.
Zum Beispiel Herbst: die Wälder legen
den Kopfschmuck an und wandern aus.

Ich war mal in Vermont, dort ist es grün . . .

## Vermont

For instance green. A green at odds with green.
Green creeps uphill and wins itself a market;
here houses painted white go for a song.

Whoever thought this up discovers
new green for instance in perpetual
instalments, never repeats himself.

Tools lie around, all greenly overcome
though rust had been their reddest resolution,
iron when formed, now to be bought as scrap.

We burned our way through woods, but the new green
grew far too fast, much faster than
and greener than for instance red.

When this same green is broken up.
For instance autumn: the woods put on
their head adornments and migrate.

Once I was in Vermont, there it is green  . . .

# Falsche Schönheit

Diese Stille,
    also der abseits in sich verbissne Verkehr,
        gefällt mir,
und dieses Hammelkotelett,
    wenn es auch kalt mittlerweile und talgig,
        schmeckt mir,
das Leben,
    ich meine die Spanne seit gestern bis Montag früh,
        macht wieder Spass:
ich lache über Teltower Rübchen,
unser Meerschweinchen erinnert mich rosa,
Heiterkeit will meinen Tisch überschwemmen,
und ein Gedanke,
    immerhin ein Gedanke,
        geht ohne Hefe auf;
           und ich freue mich,
               weil er falsch ist und schön.

## Wrong Beauty

This quiet,
    that is, the traffic some way off, its teeth stuck into itself,
        pleases me,
and this lamb cutlet,
    though cold by now and greasy,
        tastes good,
life,
    I mean the period from yesterday to Monday morning,
        is fun again:
I laugh at the dish of parsnips,
our guinea pig pinkly reminds me,
cheerfulness threatens to flood my table,
and an idea,
    an idea of sorts,
        rises without yeast;
          and I'm happy
            because it is wrong and beautiful.

# März

Schon wieder mischen sie Beton.
Von rostiger Armierung taut
die letzte Hemmung, Fertigteile
verfügen sich und stehen stramm:
Komm. Pass dich an. Komm. Pass dich an.
  Als meine Wut den Horizont verbog,
  als ich den Müll nicht schlucken wollte,
  als ich mit kleinen spitzen Verben
  Bereifung schlitzte,—Warum parken Sie?—
  als ich den Pudding durch ein Haarsieb hetzte
  und ihm sein rosa Gegenteil bewies,
  als ich mir Schatten fing, als Schattenfänger
  bezahlt, danach veranlagt wurde,
  als ich die Nägel himmelwärts
  durch frischgestrichne Bänke trieb,
  als ich Papier, mit Hass bekritzelt,
  zu Schiffchen faltete und schwimmen liess,
  als Liebe einen Knochen warf
  und meine Zunge sich Geschmack erdachte,
  als ich beschloss, die Gürtelrose zu besprechen,
  nur weil im Welken noch drei Gramm Genuss,
  als ich, es nieselte, die Bronze leckte
  und schwellenscheu die Fotzen heilig sprach,
  als meine Finger läufig wurden
  und längs den Buden jedes Astloch deckten,
  als ich die Automaten, bis game over,
  bei kleinen Stössen Klingeln lehrte,
  als jede Rechnung unterm Strich
  auf minus neunundsechzig zählte,
  als ich bei Tauben lag und schwören musste:
  Nie wieder werde ich mit Möwen!—
  als ich ein Ohr besprang, um Ablass bat:

# March

Again they're mixing concrete now.
From rusty armatures the last
small inhibition thaws, spare parts
stand at attention, fit for use:
Come on. Adapt. Come on. Adapt.
    When my great fury twisted the horizon,
    when I refused to swallow garbage,
    when with my little pointed verbs
    I slit the tyres,—why are you parking here?—
    when through a hair sieve I made the pudding squelch
    and gave it proof of its pink opposite,
    when I caught shadows and, remunerated,
    was taxed for it, profession: shadow-catcher,
    when heavenward I drove my nails
    through newly painted garden seats,
    when I took paper scribbled full of hate,
    folded it into boats and launched them,
    when love chucked me a bone, and then
    my tongue devised a relish for its taste,
    when I decided to cure shingles with a spell
    since even detumescence gives three grammes of pleasure,
    when—on a drizzly day—I licked the bronze
    and, shy of thresholds, canonized all cunts,
    when my ten fingers suddenly were in rut
    and served each knot-hole in that row of shacks,
    when, till game over, with little tilts and pushes
    I taught the slot machines to ring,
    when every bill beneath the line
    came out as minus nine pounds ten,
    when with the doves I lay and had to vow:
    never again I'll do it with the seagulls!—
    mounted an ear and begged for mercy, wheedling:

Zu trocken sind die Engel und zu eng!—
als nur noch Kopfstand mir Vokabeln gab:
Ich liebe dich. Ich liebe dich.—
Als Winterfutter aus den Mänteln
geknöpft und eingemottet wurde,
als sich das Treibhaus bunt erbrach,—
Lautsprecher in den März gestellt,—
als Kitzel Krätze Fisch und Lauch
sich stritten, brach der Frühling aus:
Ich hab genug. Komm. Zieh dich aus.

Too dry the angels are, too tight!—
when only headstands yielded phrases still:
I love you, dear. I love you, dear.—
When winter linings were unbuttoned
from overcoats and, moth-proofed, put away,
when garishly the greenhouse puked,—
loudspeaker blaring into March,—
when tickle scratches fish and leek
began to quarrel, spring broke out:
Come on now. Get undressed, girl. Quick.